Nature Science

**SHAR LEVINE
& LESLIE JOHNSTONE**

Illustrated by Dave Garbot

Sterling Publishing Co., Inc.
New York

For Sarah Hamblin. Thanks for being a part of our family for the last 15 years.—S. L.
To Jane Slater, for all her kind words and deeds.—L. J.

Project photography by Stephen Ogilvy
Other photographs by the authors or as noted.

Library of Congress Cataloging-in-Publication Data

Levine, Shar, 1953-
  Backyard science / Shar Levine & Leslie Johnstone.
     p. cm.
  Includes bibliographical references and index.
  ISBN 1-4027-1519-6 (alk. paper)
  1. Science—Experiments—Juvenile literature. I. Johnstone, Leslie. II.
Title.
Q182.3.L374 2005
507'.8—dc22

                                   2004026753

               10 9 8 7 6 5 4 3 2 1

Previously published under the title *Backyard Science.*
Published in paperback in 2007 by Sterling Publishing Co., Inc.
387 Park Avenue South, New York, NY 10016
©2005 by Shar Levine and Leslie Johnstone
Distributed in Canada by Sterling Publishing
℅ Canadian Manda Group, 165 Dufferin Street
Toronto, Ontario, Canada M6K 3H6
Distributed in the United Kingdom by GMC Distribution Services
Castle Place, 166 High Street, Lewes, East Sussex, England BN7 1XU
Distributed in Australia by Capricorn Link (Australia) Pty. Ltd.
P.O. Box 704, Windsor, NSW 2756, Australia

Printed in China

Sterling ISBN-13: 978-1-4027-1519-8 Hardcover
ISBN-10: 1-4027-1519-6
ISBN-13: 978-1-4027-4516-4 Paperback
ISBN-10: 1-4027-4516-8

For information about custom editions, special sales, or
premium and corporate purchases, please contact Sterling Special
Sales Department at 800-805-5489 or specialsales@sterlingpub.com.

Contents

Introduction

You probably think the great outdoors is a perfect place to play catch, jump rope, or have a game of tag, but did you know it's also a wonderful science laboratory? Look outside. Depending on where you live, you may see tall green leafy trees, spicy-smelling pines, or even spiky cactus plants. No matter where you live, in a city or in the country, interesting things are all around you.

Even if the weather is too cold to go outside or so hot that you may want to stay indoors, you can still have fun with the activities in this book. In fact, some of the activities are even better when you try them in the comfort of your home. If you live in an apartment or your home doesn't have a backyard, don't fret! There's probably a park or other public space where you can gather the materials needed for the activities.

You won't need anything dangerous to do these exciting science experiments. Even so, your mom, dad, or another helpful adult should read each experiment with you and help you with all the steps. They will have as much fun as you do performing the activities. Wear old clothes; some activities may be messy.

You're ready to become a backyard scientist, so grab a hat and some sunscreen if it's a sunny day, or a warm sweater if it's windy, and let's get started!

Gregor Mendel, Famous Backyard Scientist

Did you know the outdoors is one of the best places to learn about science? Many famous scientists got their start in their own backyards. Gregor Mendel (1822 to 1884) was a monk who lived in a monastery in Austria. His love of gardening and his curiosity led him to research the way that garden pea plants grew. To study how plants pass on certain physical traits (such as their height and the color or shape of their seeds) to the next generation of plants, he experimented with 28,000 pea plants. He bred plants that had different traits with each other and recorded what he noticed about the new plants that grew from their seeds. Mendel's work eventually gave rise to the science of heredity, the study of how the traits of living things are passed on to their offspring. His work was so important that he is sometimes called the father of modern genetics.

NOTE TO PARENTS AND TEACHERS

Children learn best when they are actively involved in an activity. This book is designed to help them begin to discover some very basic scientific principles. Some activities are perfect for a child to perform while you are gardening, or even while you are out on a walk. Teachers will enjoy this book as many of the activities can be done in a classroom setting. There are no expensive materials to purchase.

Adult supervision is required, as children may not understand all the instructions in the book. It is important to tell your budding scientist that observation is a perfectly

acceptable way to learn about something; all things need not be touched or probed to discover how they work.

While most homes are childproofed, the outdoors tends to be more uncontrolled. Some places have potentially dangerous creatures or plants. Closely supervise children and make sure they don't try to pick up snakes or collect stinging nettles. Some areas have dangerous spiders or scorpions. Plants like poison ivy can cause a rash if touched, so be sure children learn to recognize and avoid them. Extreme caution must be exercised when working in the garden in order to avoid these hazards. We can't stress enough the importance of going over the safety rules that follow with your child, as well as close supervision to ensure these rules are not broken.

Common flowers such as the rhododendron, poinsettia, daffodil, oleander, and even the lovely sweet pea can make you really sick if you eat them. In fact there are over 700 kinds of plants that are considered unsafe for people or animals to eat. Make sure children understand this.

SAFETY FIRST!

It's great to have fun and experiment, but there are some simple rules to follow so you won't hurt yourself or someone else. If you aren't sure if something is alright to do, ask an adult. Your adult supervisor, whether it's a parent, teacher, or babysitter, will be able to help you with the activities. Here are some things you need to know before you get started.

Do's

1. Make sure an adult is with you to supervise you while you do the experiments.
2. Wear sunscreen and protective clothing when doing the activities outdoors. Do not go outside during windstorms or when there is lightning.

3. Make sure you have on an appropriate bug spray to keep away mosquitoes.
4. Tell an adult immediately if you or someone else is hurt in any way.
5. Have an adult read all the instructions for an experiment with you before you begin any of the steps.
6. Have an adult help you gather all the materials you need for your activities.
7. Help clean up after you have finished each activity, and remember to wash your hands when you are finished with your activities.
8. Safely dispose of your experiments. Ask an adult to explain how to do this, rather than just dumping something down the sink or toilet or throwing it in the garbage.

Don'ts

1. Do not touch any creature or plant without an adult's permission. If the adult is unsure if the plant or creature is safe, just observe it.
2. Do not taste, eat, or drink any of the experiments or materials. Do not feed any experiments to anyone else, including pets.
3. Be sure that any materials you store are clearly labeled so no one mistakes them for food.
4. Do not substitute other materials for the ones listed in the book.

5. If you have allergies to any plants, flowers, or pollen, do not handle those materials. If you have asthma and are taking medication, make sure an adult carries your medicine when you are outdoors.
6. When you are outdoors, don't get too close to any creatures that can sting or bite.
7. Don't be cruel to any living creature.

MATERIALS

Below are materials and equipment that will be used in many projects. See each project for its particular materials list, and assemble all your materials before you start a project.

- clean rags
- knife
- large jar for water

- magnifying glass
- measuring cup
- measuring spoons
- mixing spoon
- old newspapers
- paper cups
- paper towels
- pencil
- plastic containers

- plastic sandwich bags
- sand shovel or trowel
- scissors
- small notebook
- tape measure
- tweezers
- twine or thin string
- watch
- waterproof marker

GLOSSARY When we introduce a new word, it will be listed in **bold** type. You will find its definition at the back of the book in the glossary.

Bath Time

At the end of a hot summer's day, it's nice to hop into a cool bath or take a refreshing shower. You can scrub away the sweat, dirt, and grunge that is covering every part of your body. But how do other creatures clean themselves?

🐞 WHAT YOU NEED

- 2 large, heavy flowerpots, about 9" (23 cm) wide*
- flowerpot saucer, about 12" to 15" (30 to 38 cm) wide
- container with water

*Note: If you don't have any heavy flowerpots, look for a large tree stump or another raised surface to use as a base. Use the lid from a garbage can or a large flat pan instead of a saucer as the container for water.

WHAT YOU DO

1. Find a flat surface close to trees or bushes to build your birdbath. Place one pot upside down on the ground. This is your base.

2. Balance the second pot, right-side up, on the first pot. Place the saucer on top of the second pot. You've made a birdbath.

3. Fill the saucer with cool water. (You will need to empty the saucer every other day and refill it with fresh water. This will keep the water clean and stop mosquitoes from laying eggs in the water.)

4. Stand behind a tree or bush or go indoors and look out a window to see who uses your birdbath.

WHAT HAPPENED

Many kinds of bird were probably attracted to your birdbath. Some birds splashed themselves in the water, while others may have just swooped down for a cool drink. Many birds also use water for making mud for their nests. Other animals may have visited your birdbath for a drink of water too.

Did You Know?

What do birds do without freshwater? The albatross, a bird that lives on the ocean, can drink seawater, which is salty. People and animals can't normally drink salty water because it makes them sick, but albatrosses have special structures near their nasal (nose) area that remove the salt from the water.

Birds of a Feather

Birds are covered with feathers. Some birds have beautiful, colorful plumage; others have gray, black, or drab coverings. Peacocks have long iridescent feathers that fan out from their tails. Swans have graceful white feathers that look like they've been put through the wash with bleach. But are all feathers the same?

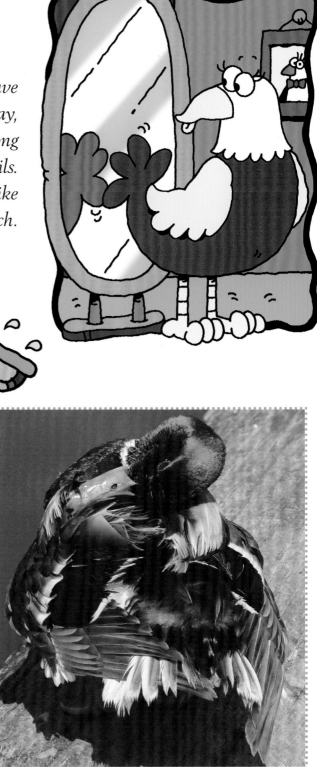

WHAT YOU NEED

- several feathers, including a down feather, long feathers, and small feathers
- newsprint paper
- sealable plastic bags
- magnifying glass
- notebook and pencil
- marker that writes on plastic
- paper
- adult helper

WHAT YOU DO

1. Look around the yard or have an adult take you for a feather-hunting walk. Gather any feathers that have fallen on the ground. If you can't find any feathers, visit a pet store and ask the staff if you can have some feathers from the bottoms of birdcages, or get some from a craft store. Try to get a variety of sizes and shapes.

A good view of a duck's wing and tail feathers.

2. As you pick up each of the feathers, place it in a plastic bag. If you know what kind of bird the feather is from, use a marker to label the bag with the name of the bird. Otherwise label it with the name of the place you found the feather.

3. Remove the feather from the bag and place it on a piece of paper. Use a magnifying glass to study the feather. Compare your feather to the ones shown and described here. What kinds of feathers have you found?

Looking at a flight feather.

4. Use a magnifying glass to study a feather. Feel the feathers. Which are strongest? Take a large feather with a central shaft. Try pulling the sides of the feather apart gently, and then push them back together.

5. Use soap and water to clean any surface on which a feather has been placed, and wash your hands after returning the feathers to their bags.

WHAT HAPPENED

The feathers did not look or feel the same. You may have found some feathers like the ones in the photos. Each kind of feather helps the bird in a special way. **Flight feathers** are big and strong. They help the bird to fly. They are found on the bird's wings and tail. They have a hollow central **shaft** and strong **vanes** (the feathery parts on each side of the shaft). **Contour feathers** are the feathers that cover most of the bird's body and give the bird its color. They have a hollow central shaft and a tapering vane that grows from each side of the shaft. They are fuzzy at the base.

Both contour and flight feathers have a vane that is made from parallel rows of branches off the shaft called barbs. The **barbs** have even smaller branches called **barbules,** which are held together by tiny hooklike barbicels. The **barbicels** hold the parts of the feather in shape. When you pulled the feather apart and pushed it together again, the barbicels came undone and then reattached to each other.

Down feathers are soft and fuzzy; they grow underneath the contour feathers and keep the bird warm. Down feathers are simpler than contour feathers and don't have barbicels.

Semiplume feathers are fuzzy but are larger than down feathers, with a large central shaft. They help to keep the bird warm also. **Filoplumes** are very tiny thin feathers with a single shaft and a small or missing vane section. Birds use filoplumes to sense movement. Feathers are made from a substance called keratin, the same material used to make our hair and fingernails.

TRY THIS

The next time you are near a lake or stream, see if you can find any ducks. Watch the ducks as they use their beaks to nibble on their feathers. They are squeezing oil into their feathers to help them to stay dry and buoyant in the water. In fact, birds spend a great deal of time preening, or cleaning their feathers. They need to align the barbs in their contour and flight feathers so that they mesh together nicely and become a solid surface to push against the air when the bird is flying.

Preening duck, arranging contour feathers.

Did You Know?

Today only birds have feathers, but scientists have found fossils of dinosaurs that were covered with feathers. They are still trying to figure out how birds evolved, perhaps from dinosaurs.

Bird Nests & Houses

Birds don't have special tools for constructing their nests. They use twigs, sticks, mud, moss, feathers, and whatever else they can find to make a cozy place to lay their eggs. No one teaches them how to construct a nest; they are born with this knowledge. Can we build a nest? Let's see if we can learn how. Birds need places to nest, so let's make a simple birdhouse for them too.

WHAT YOU NEED

- clean plastic gallon (3.8 L) jug from milk or juice, with cap
- knife
- waterproof tape like strapping tape or duct tape
- branch about ½" (1 cm) thick and 12" (30 cm) long, for perch
- rope or thick cord, 6' to 10' (1.8 m to 3 m) long
- pencil
- moss
- old newspapers and clean rags
- twigs
- string
- egg
- scissors
- leaves
- mud (optional)
- adult helper

WHAT YOU DO

1. Look around outside. Can you see any nests? Take a walk with an adult helper. Check in the branches of trees. If you live near a forest, check for holes in trees. Some birds build their nests inside these hollows. If you live near a lake, you might even find a nest hidden in tall reeds or bushes. It's best to look for nests in the fall. In the spring, you could disturb nesting birds, who might leave their eggs. Be sure not to touch the nest, or you will disturb the birds. On your trip, you may get ideas as to how birds' nests are made and what materials birds use.

Otherwise, look in a book about birds for more information.

2. Take the twigs, straw, string, paper, moss, and leaves, and try to make your own bird's nest from them. Use mud if you want to. Can you get your materials to hold together in a bowl shape? How sturdy is your nest? Will it hold an egg?

Eagle's nest.

Ducks use down feathers to line their nests.

3. Make a house for birds in your backyard. Have an adult cut a small round hole, about 1" to 2" (2.5 to 5 cm) across, in one side of the milk jug. Center the hole in the middle of one of the sides of the jug and position it about 2" (5 cm) from the bottom of jug (see photo). Wrap some tape around the edges of the hole to make a smooth opening.

4. Rip up a page or two of newspaper and put the shredded paper in the bottom of the jug. You can use a pencil or chopstick to push the paper into the hole. You can also use some moss or even ripped-up rags to line the bottom of the birdhouse. Put the cap on the jug.

5. Have an adult cut 2 small holes for a perch, one near the bottom of the entrance and the other on the opposite side of the jug. Push the thin branch through these holes to make a perch for the birds.

6. Choose a safe place, away from fences, to hang the birdhouse. Have an adult use the rope to hang the birdhouse in an area where cats can't reach it.

7. Observe your birdhouse from time to time to see who has moved in.

Nest Trivia

■ *The tailorbird of Southeast Asia is well named. It actually sews leaves together with plant fiber, using its bill as a needle.*

■ *Have you ever seen bird's nest soup listed on the menu of a Chinese restaurant? It turns out there is truth in advertising. This delicacy is made from the nest of the swiftlet of Southeast Asia. The nest, made from the bird's hardened saliva, is edible.*

■ *Do you have dried flowers in your bathroom to make it smell nice? It turns out that some birds also like potpourri. On an island in the Mediterranean called Corsica, the Blue Tit uses up to 10 fragrant plants, including lavender and mint, to line its nest. Scientists think that the birds do this to keep bugs and parasites away from their chicks.*

■ *After the leaves have fallen from the trees, it's easy to see bird nests. Some birds build new nests each year. Others, like eagles, may return to the same nest year after year.*

WHAT HAPPENED

You probably learned some good ways of shaping twigs into a nest, but it may not have been as well made as a bird's nest. If your nest had a hollow in the center, you might have been able to put an egg in it. The birdhouse wasn't hard to make. After watching your birdhouse for a while, you may have found that some birds have come to live in it.

Did You Know?

Not all birds like the same kind of doors on their houses. Small birds like houses with small openings, while larger birds like wider openings. The size of the hole you make for your feathered friends will help determine what kind of bird will nest there. Small birds like chickadees, wrens, and swallows generally like openings that are between 1 and 1½" (2.5 to 3.5 cm) wide.

Stronger Than You Think

When you buy eggs in the grocery store, they come packaged in sturdy Styrofoam or cardboard containers. The eggs must be handled gently so they don't break. But are eggs really fragile? Let's see.

WHAT YOU NEED

- 4 uncooked eggs
- egg carton
- heavy book, about 2 lbs (1 kg)

WHAT YOU DO

1. Place an egg with the pointy part down in each of 4 spaces in the carton. Arrange the eggs so the distance between them is about an inch (2.5 cm) less than the length of the book on the long side.

2. Gently place the book on the eggs. Do not drop the book onto the eggs. Did the eggs break? Take the book off and put the eggs back in the refrigerator. Wash your hands with soap and water after you have handled the eggs.

WHAT HAPPENED

The weight of the book didn't break the eggs, because it pressed down from the top. The ends of the egg are shaped like domes. This dome shape is what makes the eggshell hard to break. When you press on the top of the egg, the force you apply is spread out evenly around the eggshell so that no single point supports the whole force.

Did You Know?

Eggs are so perfect that an engineer might have designed them. Because of their oval shape, eggs can't roll far from the nest. They wobble when they roll and make small circles. When you look at a hen incubating her eggs, it looks like she is sitting on them. That isn't what is really going on underneath her feathers. Despite the fact that the eggs can support a lot of weight on the dome, the bird can't guarantee that they will be pointing the right way up. The hen makes sure that the eggs don't get crushed by squatting to hold up her weight. The eggs fit into the area formed by her legs and her belly.

Hum Along

Why do hummingbirds hum? Don't they know the words? In reality, hummingbirds don't hum. The humming noise they make comes from their rapid wingbeat. Unlike other birds, who dine on seeds and grains, these energetic creatures only eat nectar, so feeding hummingbirds is a good thing.

 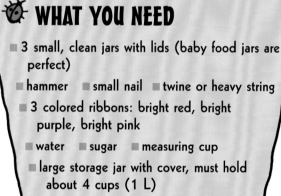

WHAT YOU NEED

- 3 small, clean jars with lids (baby food jars are perfect)
- hammer ■ small nail ■ twine or heavy string
- 3 colored ribbons: bright red, bright purple, bright pink
- water ■ sugar ■ measuring cup
- large storage jar with cover, must hold about 4 cups (1 L)
- mixing spoon
- adult helper

WHAT YOU DO

1. Remove the lid of each small jar and place it on a work table with the top facing up. Have an adult use the hammer and nail to poke several holes in each of the lids, from the outside in. Then turn the lid over and hammer down the sharp edges of the holes made by the nail, as these could hurt the hummingbird.

2. Dissolve 1 cup (250 mL) of sugar in 4 cups of water. Mix well with the spoon. This liquid will serve as the hummingbird's **nectar**. Nectar is the sweet juice that flowers make to attract insects and birds. Do not use honey or artificial sweeteners.

3. Fill the 3 jars about three-fourths of the way with the liquid, and replace the lids, closing them tightly. Place the leftover nectar in the storage jar, and store it in the fridge. Do not leave it unrefrigerated

4. Tie a long piece of string or twine around the neck of each of the containers. The string is what you will use to tie each feeder to a tree.

5. Tie one colored ribbon around each of the feeders.

6. Have an adult help you hang each of the containers in a safe place in the garden, where cats can't reach, and preferably somewhere where there is some shade. When hung, the container should tip forward a little, allowing the bird to reach the nectar.

7. Every 5 days or so, take down the feeders and wash the containers and lids. Refill the nectar and re-hang the feeders. It's important to keep the nectar clean.

8. Watch the feeder for hummingbirds. Which feeder are the birds most attracted to? If you wish, try changing the ribbon colors after a while.

WHAT HAPPENED

Hummingbirds loved the sugar water. They were attracted to the bright colors of the ribbons. The birds usually are most attracted to the purple and red ribbons and less attracted to the pink ribbon. You may have noticed that these tiny birds beat their wings so quickly that they almost seem to disappear. Their wings beat about 78 times  per second normally, but they can beat up to 200 times per second.

Night Shift

What happens in your yard at night when you are asleep? Are there creatures that visit and traipse through your garden? Here's a way to find out what happened in the night.

WHAT YOU NEED

- soft earth or sand, about 4 lbs (2 kg)
- tray or flat container for sand (optional)
- scoop or shovel to dig up earth or sand
- water
- small container

WHAT YOU DO

1. Look around the flower beds in your yard or another area where there is soft soil. See if you can spot any marks in the soil that look like animal footprints.

2. If the sand or earth is dry, add some water to it so it becomes damp. Leave the dampened sand or soft dampened earth spread out overnight in a place where you think animals may go. Put it in a tray if you wish. Put a small container of water nearby to attract animals.

3. In the morning, look at the sand or earth. If there are any footprints, compare them to the footprints shown here to see if you can identify the animal that made the prints. You may have to do some more research. See if there is a field guide to animal tracks in your local library, or look on the Internet.

4. If no animal tracks appear, try moving the experiment to another part of your yard.

5. If you don't live in a house with a yard, look at the soft soil in the park or schoolyard to see if there are any animal footprints.

WHAT HAPPENED

Not all animals are active during the day. Many come out at night. Some animals may have walked on your earth or sand at night when they came to get a drink. Depending on where you live, there could be raccoons, skunks, bears, or even the family cat or dog. Some yards have visits from deer, chipmunks, squirrels, or other small rodents.

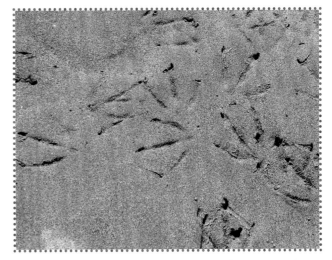

Heron tracks

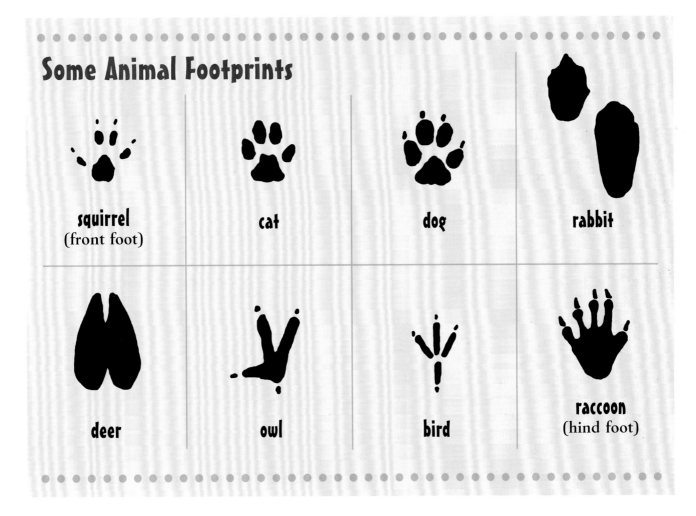

Some Animal Footprints

squirrel (front foot)

cat

dog

rabbit

deer

owl

bird

raccoon (hind foot)

Worm Roundup

Earthworms are probably the easiest creatures to catch and to study. Earthworms won't bite you because they don't have teeth. They won't sting you because they don't have stingers. They aren't endangered, so handling them isn't a bad thing. And best of all, they are all over the place. No matter where you live, you probably will find one of these wonderful crawlers near you. Here are some easy ways to collect worms. Keep the worms in a dark, damp place. Then use them for the next activity, Worm Sounds.

WHAT YOU NEED

- small shovel or trowel
- plastic bag
- flashlight
- square of red cellophane to fit over flashlight
- masking tape or cellophane tape
- jar half-filled with damp earth, with lid
- magnifying glass
- old battery-operated toothbrush (optional)
- damp cloth or paper towel
- adult helper

WHAT YOU DO

There are several ways to find worms. Use any of the ones given here.

1. Take a walk in the garden in the evening or early morning. Have an adult help you turn over some rocks or leaves or dig up the earth. Gather up a big, juicy earthworm

with a plastic bag and gently place it in the jar of damp earth.

2. Here's another way to find worms. Tape red cellophane over the glass of the flashlight. In the evening, find a wet spot on your lawn and look for a small mound of dirt. This is a worm burrow. Sit very still and shine the flashlight onto the hole. Wait till the worm crawls out, and gently pick it up.

3. At dusk, find a damp area on a lawn that has been freshly mowed or raked. Stand on this spot and stomp your feet up and down in a rhythmic beat. Have a friend or helper look for the worms you bring to the surface.

4. If you have an old battery-operated toothbrush, here's an interesting use for it. Place the toothbrush on the ground near a worm burrow and turn it on. See if the vibrations bring the worm to the surface.

5. After you get your worm, place it on a damp cloth or paper towel and use your magnifying glass to take a close look at the creature. Treat the worm gently.

WHAT HAPPENED

Using one of these methods, you managed to attract some worms. Earthworms belong to a group of animals called **annelids,** or segmented worms. They have segments or ringlike parts that are attached together. You may have seen your worm wriggling. Worms move by contracting their muscles, which pull them along the ground. No matter how closely you look at a worm, you won't be able to tell if it's a boy or a girl. Worms have both male and female parts at the same time.

Did You Know?

After a summer rain, look outside on the sidewalk. You may see many worms crawling along the pavement. But what makes the worms leave their safe place in the ground and seek the wide open spaces? Worms don't have lungs, like people do. Lungs put oxygen into your blood and take out carbon dioxide, a waste product. Instead, a worm has to rely on its skin for breathing. If the soil that the worm is in gets too wet, the worm will move up to the surface to get more oxygen.

Worm Sounds

On a nice grassy area, put your ear to the ground. What do you hear? Do you hear the worms munching their way through the soil? Probably not. But what noise does an earthworm make?

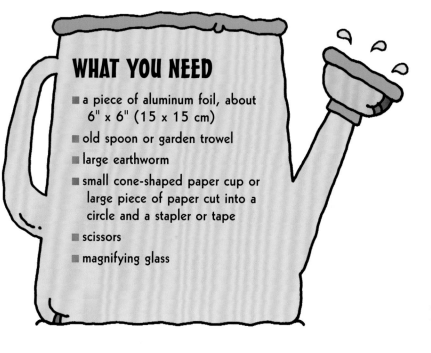

WHAT YOU NEED

- a piece of aluminum foil, about 6" x 6" (15 x 15 cm)
- old spoon or garden trowel
- large earthworm
- small cone-shaped paper cup or large piece of paper cut into a circle and a stapler or tape
- scissors
- magnifying glass

WHAT YOU DO

1. Using any of the techniques in Worm Roundup, find a big fat worm, or use the worms you already found.

2. Place the aluminum foil square in a shaded spot. Gently put the worm on the foil. Do not place the foil in a sunny spot as the heat from the sun will harm the worm.

3. Listen closely. Can you hear the worm moving across the surface of the foil?

4. Cut off the pointed tip of a cone-shaped paper cup, or make a cone of paper out of a large paper circle by cutting it and folding it into a cone, and stapling it to hold it together. Place the narrow end of the cone near your ear and hold the wide end close to the worm. Does this make it easier to hear the worm move?

5. Gently turn the worm over. Use a magnifying glass to look at the bristles (**setae**) on the bottom of the worm. What do they look like? Touch the worm gently with your finger in a few places.

6. Return the worm to the earth in a damp place.

WHAT HAPPENED

The worm made a scratchy sound as it moved across the foil. This is because the worm has bristles or **setae** underneath, which help it grip the sides of the tunnels under the ground where it lives. You may have been able to hear the sound of the worm moving better when you used the paper cone, because the shape of the cone directed more sound into your ear. You saw by the way the worm reacted to touch that certain parts of the worm are more sensitive than others. Worms like the feeling of solid walls, such as the sides of the tunnels that they dig in the earth. They will move around until they find a wall; then they will stay still.

DID YOU KNOW?

Imagine a worm twice as long as your bicycle. If you lived in Australia, you might dig up one of these Gippsland earthworms, the largest worms in the world.

Snail Trail

How would you like to carry your home with you everywhere? You could simply curl up in your warm safe place whenever you wanted to and read a good book. Let's meet an animal that does take its house everywhere it goes. If you live in a damp area, you can find snails in gardens, on trees, in ponds, and even in the ocean. Pick up the first garden snail you see and try this.

WHAT YOU NEED

- land snail from garden
- plastic bag
- spatula or sand shovel
- transparent plastic container or jar
- paper towel
- parsley, celery, or lettuce
- piece of apple
- green leaves and stems
- magnifying glass
- flashlight
- plant mister with cool water
- saucer

WHAT YOU DO

1. Look in the garden under leaves or on trees to find a snail. If you live in a damp area, you may find some. Pick up the snail by its shell with your hands, or use a plastic bag or a spatula to lift the snail up, and place it in a container. If the snail is on a stem, just take the whole stem; don't try to pull the snail off.

2. Use your magnifying glass to take a close look at the snail. Does it seem to be looking or feeling around? What does the bottom of the snail look like? Shine the flashlight on the snail. How does it react? If you have trouble getting your snail to come out of its shell, try quickly dipping the shell into a small saucer of cool water or spraying the snail with water from the mister.

WHAT HAPPENED

If you look at the food, you might see tiny scratches or munched-away areas where the snail has been eating. These marks were made by the snail's teeth. Unlike people, a snail has a special structure called the **radula** inside its mouth that is spiral-shaped or coiled and has thousands of teeth along its surface. The teeth scrape away food.

As you may have seen, when the snail goes into its shell, it closes off the bottom, sealing out the world. This protects the snail's body from drying up when the weather is dry, and it keeps the snail from being eaten. When you sprayed it with mist or dunked it in water, the snail came out and became active again. When you shined the light at the snail, it may have moved in the direction of the light to see what was happening or away from the light if it was too bright.

Did You Know?

Snails belong to a class of animals called **gastropods,** which means "stomach-foot" in Greek. A snail moves along by using the muscular foot on the underside of its body. It glides slowly on this foot by waves of muscle movement. It leaves a mucus trail on things it walks on, which helps it to slide.

3. Put a piece of fresh parsley, celery, or lettuce near the snail. Listen closely. Can you hear the snail munching away on this treat? Try giving it a piece of apple. Hold the container above you so you can watch the snail move and eat.

4. Return the snail to the garden where you found it when you are finished with this activity.

Slug Slime

If you live in Northern California or the Pacific Northwest, you are probably familiar with the giant banana slug, which looks like an alien creature with its long tentacles and spotted green slimy body. Are slugs simply snails who have lost their homes? Yes, in a way. Let's take a closer peek at slugs.

WHAT YOU NEED

- a slug—the bigger, the better
- small plastic bag
- sand shovel
- clear plastic container
- craft stick
- piece of paper
- pencil
- different kinds of glue or glue sticks
- dried pasta, like bowties or macaroni
- magnifying glass

WHAT YOU DO

1. The best place to find a slug is in the garden or in wet, moist areas in the yard. Look under logs or on garden paths in the evening. If you wish, use a sand shovel or small plastic bag to gently scoop up the slug and place it in a clear plastic container. Use a magnifying glass to take a close look at the slug. Can you identify the slug's eyes? They're at the end of long, antenna-like tentacles.

2. Hold the container so you can see the surface under the slug as it moves along. You should see thick slime left by the slug.

3. Use a craft stick to scrape up some of the slime. Spread the slime on a piece of paper and place several pieces of pasta on the slug slime. Write SLIME near the pasta that was glued with slug slime.

4. Smear some store-bought glues on the piece of paper and stick some pasta to each glue smear. With your pencil, note on the paper which glue you used in each place. Allow the glues to dry thoroughly.

5. When the glues are dry, lift up the paper. Does the pasta stick to the slug slime? Do the other glues hold the pasta on the paper?

6. When you have finished gathering the slime from the slug, return the slug to the garden and wash your hands.

WHAT HAPPENED

Like snails, slugs are gastropods. A slug moves along by the muscular foot on the underside of its body. It travels slowly on this foot, using waves of muscle movement to glide along. The slime that slugs produce is a **lubricant,** a substance that makes a surface slippery, which helps them slide along.

The slime also keeps their skin moist, which is important because, like worms, slugs breathe through their skin. The slime protects slugs from predators, because many animals that might want to eat slugs find the slime disgusting. It contains a chemical which, when eaten, makes a **predator's** mouth feel numb. Slime doesn't make a particularly good glue compared to store-bought glues, so you probably found that the pasta fell off the slime patch.

SLIMY FUTURE

Three University of Washington professors, Pedro Verdugo, Christopher Viney, and Ingrith Deyrup-Olsen, have been studying the mucus of the common banana slug. They have discovered that the mucus has some special qualities. When water is added to it, the slug slime can absorb up to 100 times its own initial volume in water. The slime acts like a giant sponge, sucking up water to keep the slug moist. The researchers can see several possible future uses for slug slime technology, including traps for pollutants in sewage treatment plants and water-based lubricants.

Catch a Web

If you take a walk early in the morning, you can't help notice how spider webs seem to shimmer with dew. Wouldn't it be nice to capture that beauty? Here's a way to appreciate spider webs and create a piece of art for your room.

WHAT YOU NEED

- spider web
- paper or notebook
- pencil
- adult helper

WHAT YOU DO

1. Take along an adult to help you find a spider web. If you live in an area that has any dangerous spiders, like black widow spiders, take extra care when choosing a web. Look on fence posts, in spaces between trees or shrubs, and even on garden furniture.

2. Look at the web, and try to draw the shape of the web on your paper or notebook. If you see the spider, try drawing it too, in the place on the web where it is sitting.

3. Compare the web you found to the ones shown here and on page 32.

WHAT HAPPENED

You observed a spider web and drew a picture of it. Most spider webs we see in the garden are wheel-shaped webs called orb webs. Some webs are triangular and some are less-organized tangle webs. Some are sheet webs and some have a funnel or dome shape. There are also bell-shaped webs. Spiders are born knowing how to spin webs. They don't have to be taught what to do.

You may have seen the spider in its web. Spiders don't usually get caught in their own webs. Scientists think this is because they have comblike structures and oil on the bottoms of their feet, which keep them from sticking.

Orb web

Did You Know?

Spiders are not insects; instead they belong to a group of animals called **arachnids.** Spiders have 8 legs, 8 eyes, 2 main body parts, and they don't have wings. On the bottom of the back end of a spider's body there are some fingerlike structures called **spinnerets.** The spinnerets give off a liquid that becomes spider silk when it hardens in the air. The silk is used to make all the different parts of the web. The sticky kind of spider silk is used to catch insects. The nonsticky kind is used to make drop lines for when spiders go "bungee jumping" to new place on their webs.

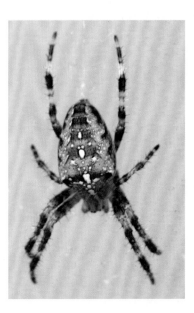

Amazing Spider Silk

What do spider webs and bulletproof vests have in common? They are both made from extremely strong fibers. Spider silk is one of the strongest materials around. It can support more weight for its size than steel. A strand of spider silk with the same diameter as a pencil would be strong enough, experts believe, to stop a Boeing 747 jet airplane in flight. It is also light and stretchable enough to make delicate webs. The material currently used to make most bulletproof vests is Kevlar(TM). Scientists are studying the chemical makeup of spider silk to help them improve existing synthetic fibers and to discover new ones.

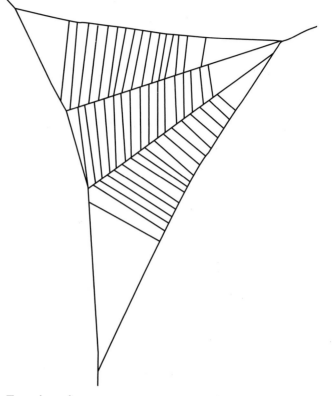

Triangle web

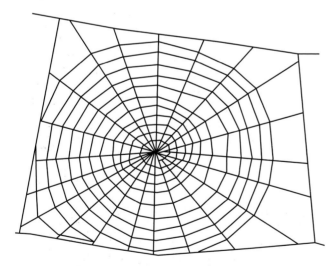

Orb web

Tangle web

Hi, Butterfly

How would you like to keep butterflies, even in the winter? Here's a way to capture your own butterfly without harming one of nature's most beautiful creatures.

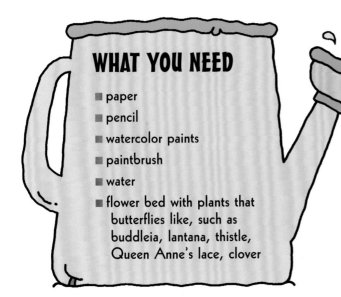

WHAT YOU NEED

- paper
- pencil
- watercolor paints
- paintbrush
- water
- flower bed with plants that butterflies like, such as buddleia, lantana, thistle, Queen Anne's lace, clover

WHAT YOU DO

1. Plop yourself down in a comfy chair somewhere outside near some small, brightly colored flowers like those listed above. Sit still and see if you are visited by any butterflies. Try to notice their shape and coloring.

2. While you are waiting for a butterfly, make your own butterfly. Fold a piece of paper in half. Open it up. Use a pencil to draw the left half of the outline of a butterfly on the left side of the folded paper. See the butterfly shapes shown on page 34 for reference. The center dotted line of the drawing should be along the fold.

3. Using your watercolors, paint over the pencil outline with a dark color. Let the outline dry a little.

4. Paint blobs of color in an interesting pattern inside the butterfly outline.

5. While the paint is still wet, fold the paper closed on the crease and pat the paper flat with the palm of your hand.

6. Open the paper to reveal your butterfly. Finish the outline on the right side. Does your painting look like any butterflies you've seen?

7. To attract more butterflies to your garden, plant some of the plants that butterflies like in a sunny spot (see Butterfly Gardens on page 35).

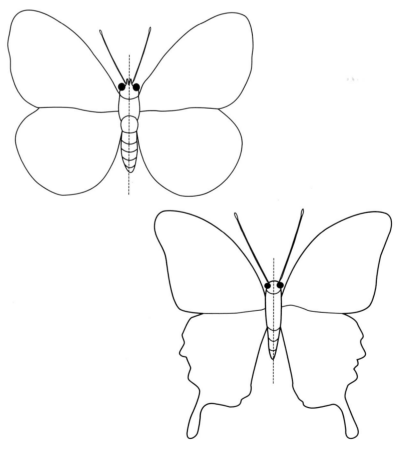

When you painted half the butterfly and folded the paper, transferring the paint to the other half across the fold, you made a reversed copy of the first half. The correspondence of shape a butterfly has is called **bilateral** (two-sided) **symmetry.** Many insects and other animals have bilateral symmetry.

Did You Know?

The bright colors and shapes on the wings of some butterflies are used for protection. Bright colors are a warning to predators that an insect is poisonous or tastes bad. Birds won't eat Monarch butterflies as they are poisonous. The patterns on some butterflies help them to blend in with their surroundings. Some wing designs look like large eyes, which mislead predators into thinking that they are looking at the eyes of a much larger animal, such as an owl, which scares them away.

Butterfly Gardens

Butterflies are attracted to small, brightly colored flowers. Nectar, a sweet liquid made by the flowers, is the butterfly's food source. A butterfly inserts its coiled, tubelike tongue, or proboscis, *into the flower to suck up the nectar. If the flower is too big, the butterfly can't reach the nectar. Particular favorites of butterflies include nasturtiums, larkspur, pennyroyal, bergamot, mint, thistles, lantana, clover, milkweed, Queen Anne's lace, and butterfly bush or buddleia.*

Some butterflies need a particular plant on which to lay their eggs. Check with a local garden center, field guide, or botanical garden to see if you can plant any of these in your garden, to make it more inviting to butterflies. Children all over the world plant butterfly gardens so butterflies will have places to feed and lay their eggs, because many butterflies are losing their habitats, *the places where they normally live.*

Becoming a Butterfly

In the beginning, people didn't know that caterpillars became butterflies. They thought they were two different animals. Today we know that the caterpillar is a larva, *a development stage of the butterfly.*

The caterpillar starts out as a tiny egg on the underside of a leaf. Then it hatches out and eats large quantities of leaves. It grows so much that it outgrows its skin and must molt, *shedding its outer layer of skin. Caterpillars molt several times as they grow larger. When the caterpillar gets large enough, it builds a cocoon or* chrysalis *around itself. The chrysalis is a strong, closed sleeping bag, which it attaches to a branch or a plant. The caterpillar becomes a* pupa, *a resting stage during which it is changing to a butterfly. Inside the chrysalis, the pupa starts changing and growing the parts of a butterfly that it didn't have before, including wings and antennae. When it is ready, the former pupa comes out of the chrysalis as a beautiful butterfly. This dramatic change from egg, to larva, to pupa, and finally to butterfly is called* metamorphosis, *which means "change of shape" in Greek.*

Ladybug Beds

Whether they are called ladybugs or ladybirds, these beautiful beetles are favorites of children everywhere. Gardeners like them too, because they eat aphids, insect pests that attack flowers and crops. Let's build a home to keep these beetles safe over the winter.

WHAT YOU NEED

- empty toilet paper roll
- clean container with a plastic lid*
- masking tape
- scissors
- duct tape
- sawdust or hamster litter
- large spoon or measuring scoop
- ladybug liquid pheromones (optional)**
- adult helper

*Note: The container that cocoa comes in is perfect.

**Available at specialty bird feed stores or pet stores.

WHAT YOU DO

1. Trim the toilet paper cardboard roll (if necessary) so that it is about an inch (2.5 cm) shorter than the container you will use.
2. Cover the opening of one end of a toilet paper roll with masking tape to close off the opening. Fill half of the toilet paper roll with

sawdust or litter. This will be the bedding for the ladybugs. Place a small piece of masking tape across the opposite, open end of the toilet paper roll, so that the tape seals about half of the opening.

3. Have an adult cut a ¼" (5 mm) wide segment off the edge of the plastic lid so beetles can get in and out (see photos).

4. Turn the container on its side. Carefully place the toilet paper roll inside of the empty container, so the sealed end of the toilet paper roll is facing towards you and the half-closed end is facing inwards, towards the back of the container.

5. Tape the toilet paper roll to the inside of the empty container. The top edge of the toilet paper roll should be even with the edge of the container.

6. If you wish, add a drop or two of ladybug pheromone to the opening of the lid. This will attract the ladybugs to their new home. If you have a plant covered with **aphids** (tiny green insect pests that suck out sap from plants) in your yard, carefully transfer a leaf from the plant into the opening of your ladybug home. This will attract ladybugs, because ladybugs eat aphids.

7. Have an adult help you find a safe place for your ladybug house. Duct-tape the container so it is lying on its side on a fence or at the corner of a garden wall between two bricks, so it doesn't roll. The opening in the lid should be facing toward the bottom. Make sure no rain can drip into the ladybug house.

WHAT HAPPENED

If you are lucky, and there are some ladybugs in your yard, you have given them a sheltered place where they can spend the winter. They will hibernate, living on their stored fat, and come out again when the weather gets warm.

Meet the Beetles

Beetles are insects with very hard outer wings and strong bodies. The beetle has a tough jointed exoskeleton *(skeleton on the outside of its body), as all insects have. The red-and-black parts of the ladybug's body are the protective outer wings that cover the more delicate hindwings underneath when the beetle isn't flying.*

Ladybugs have a life cycle that begins with an egg. The egg hatches into a grublike larva (plural = larvae). Eventually, after lots of eating, the larva changes to a pupa and goes through a resting stage, and finally it becomes the adult beetle. Beetle larvae are soft. They look like tiny alligators and don't resemble the adult beetles at all.

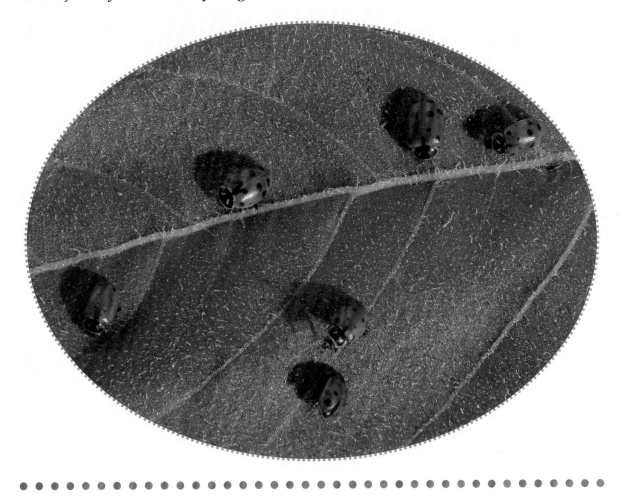

Hide & Seek

Look through your window into your backyard. If you don't have a yard, take a look in a wooded area or park. Can you see any wild creatures? (No, a pet cat or dog doesn't count.) If you are patient, you may see small birds hiding in the trees or maybe an insect sitting on a leaf. How does an animal hide in plain sight?

WHAT YOU NEED

- colored toothpicks: yellow, green, and red, about 8 of each color, or plain wooden toothpicks and yellow, red, and green paints or markers
- helpers

WHAT YOU DO

1. Find a spot with green grass. Count out 12 toothpicks, 4 of each color. (Color the toothpicks if you have plain wood-colored ones.)

2. Close your eyes and toss the toothpicks into the air. Then try to find them with your helpers. Which color toothpicks were the easiest to find? Which were the hardest?

3. Try this activity again, this time on a patch of earth. Which toothpicks were the easiest to find?

4. If you have a garden with many flowers, toss the toothpicks into a small section where there are flowers. Which toothpicks were easy to find in the flowers?

5. Throw away the toothpicks after this activity; do not put them in your mouth. Make sure you find all the toothpicks, because they will really hurt your feet if you step on them when you are barefoot.

WHAT HAPPENED

On the grass, the green toothpicks were harder to find than any other color. The red toothpicks were the easiest to find on the grass. Some of the yellow toothpicks were hard to find in the flowers, but they were easy to find on the earth. Many animals have colors and shapes that keep them from being seen by other creatures. This keeps them from being eaten. This protection is called **camouflage.** Some insects look like the leaves or twigs of the plants on which they live. Animals that live in snowy regions blend in with their surroundings by having white fur or feathers. Sloths have hair on which green algae grows, making them look green like the trees in which they live.

Camouflage

Look at the pictures shown here. Can you find the following creatures? Turtle, anole, goslings, bullfrog.

Ants on a Log

Do you like ants on a log? No, not real ants on a log, but a piece of yummy celery with a line of spreadable cheese filling the curve, plus a dotting of raisin "ants" along the cheese. What do you think real ants like to eat? Maybe you can find out.

🐞 WHAT YOU NEED

- disposable plastic or paper plate
- teaspoon
- felt marker or crayon
- small leftover food bits, like fruit, cheese vegetables, or bread
- sweet treats like candy, chocolate, or cookies
- a clove of garlic
- ant colony
- adult helper
- magnifying glass

WHAT YOU DO

1. Use a felt marker or crayon to divide a plate into eight equal pie- shaped sections.

2. Place about one teaspoon (5 mL) of each kind of food in a section. For example, put a small piece of strawberry in one section, a piece of cheese in the next section, a broken cracker in the third section, and so on until each section has a piece of food in it.

3. Place this plate near an ant colony. Have an adult help you find a good place. Stand back and observe from a safe distance. What did the ants do?

WHAT HAPPENED

You probably found that more ants crawled onto some foods than others. Ants have food preferences. Many like sweet foods the best and sour foods the least. Ants live in groups called colonies. Some of their colonies have 50,000 or even 500,000 ants. Ant colonies are like miniature cities: vast tunnels beneath the surface connect various parts of the colony. Ant highways even run between different ant nests! Once one of the ants finds a food it likes, the ant can send a message to the rest of the colony. The first ant to discover the food will lay down a chemical track back to the nest so the other ants can follow it to the food. The ants will then begin carrying back bits of food for the colony. If you look through a magnifying glass, you may see the ants communicating with each other using their antennae.

DID YOU KNOW

■ Ants are insects. Like other insects, an ant has six legs and three body parts (head, thorax, and abdomen). At some stage in their lives, some of the ants had wings, even though the worker ants you saw didn't have any wings.

■ Ants belong to the grouping Hymenoptera, the same grouping of insects as wasps and bees. Hymenoptera means "membrane wing." You may have noticed that ants have narrow waists between their second and third body parts (thorax and abdomen). Wasps have this shape also.

■ Like wasps and bees, ants can give a powerful pinch and a strong injection of venom (poison).

■ Not all ants live in nests. Army ants of the tropics in the New World and driver ants in tropical Africa are nomadic; they wander and have no permanent nests. They travel in long columns and attack and eat animals that they catch, even large animals.

■ The tunneling of ants mixes the soil and brings air into it, so most ants are helpful to humans.

Ants on a
peony bud.

Social Animals

Ants work together and so are considered social animals. Ants even have their own form of farming. One type of ant, called the Attini ant, gathers leaves. When these leaves rot, the ants use them as fertilizer to grow mushrooms. Other ants protect aphids and "milk" the aphids to get a sweet substance called honeydew. *Because ants have no plastic containers or refrigerators in which to keep their honeydew, the liquid is stored in the bodies of special worker ants, which act as containers. They release the honeydew back to the other ants when there is a shortage of food.*

Ants are very strong. An ant can carry 10 to 20 times its body weight. Ants work in teams to carry heavy things. Raising the young ants is another task that ants do together. The queen ant lays many eggs in her nest underground. After they hatch out into larvae, worker ants feed them while they are growing.

Barking Up the Wrong Tree

Feel your arm. Is it smooth and soft? If you have teenaged brother or sister, feel his or her arm. Is it as soft as yours? A tree's bark is its skin. Some trees have smooth bark; others have rough, sharp surfaces. As the tree grows, the bark has to grow, too, or the tree would burst like a balloon. Let's look at some bark without harming the tree.

WHAT YOU NEED

- a few pieces of light-colored paper
- masking tape
- crayons
- a few different kinds of tree

WHAT YOU DO

1. Find a sturdy tree and place a piece of paper flat on the tree's surface. Use masking tape to attach the paper to the tree.

2. Peel the crayon so it has no paper on it. Rub the side of a crayon up and down (not side to side) on the paper over the tree's bark until a pattern emerges.

3. Take a leaf from the tree and place the leaf on a flat surface. Tape the leaf down. Place a piece of paper over the leaf. Tape the paper down to keep it from moving. Make a rubbing of the leaf as you did with the tree bark. This will give you a matching set of rubbings for the tree.

4. Choose a different kind of tree and repeat steps 1 to 3. Do the rubbings look the same? See if people can guess which tree each rubbing came from.

WHAT HAPPENED

You got a picture of the tree's bark and its leaf. Some trees had bark that was smooth; others had a bumpier surface. As a tree ages, the bark changes. If you could compare the bark from the bottom of a tree to the bark at the top, you would find that the bark is quite different.

How Tall Am I?

What is the biggest tree that you can see? If you live in Northern California, you might say the giant sequoia is the biggest tree. If you live in Florida, you might marvel at the huge palms swaying in the wind. And if you live in the Pacific Northwest; the largest tree is the Douglas Fir. But how can you tell how tall a tree is?

WHAT YOU NEED

- trees
- protractor
- drinking straw
- masking tape
- string
- small weight such as a metal washer
- pen
- piece of tape
- helper
- long tape measure
- scissors
- pen and paper
- pebble or small stick

WHAT YOU DO

1. Tape the drinking straw to the straight side of the protractor, as shown in the photo.
2. Put a piece of tape above the line that reads 45°, so it's easy to find. Use a pen to make a line on the tape at 45°.

3. Tie one end of a piece of string to a small weight, and tie the other end to the straw right at the center of the protractor.

4. Have a helper measure your height from the eyes down using a tape measure. Write this number down.

5. Go outside and find a tree that is by itself on a flat surface, away from other trees.

6. Point one end of the drinking straw towards the tree, and move away from the tree so you can see the top of the tree through the straw when the string with the weight covers the 45° mark on your protractor. Ask your helper to move the string so it exactly covers the 45° mark.

7. Once you have moved far enough away to see the treetop, mark your place with a stick or pebble. With your helper, measure the distance from your marker to the base of the tree, using the tape measure. Write this number down.

8. Add together your height and the distance from the tree. The sum is equal to the height of the tree.

WHAT HAPPENED

You used an easy way to figure out the height of the tree. What makes this possible is the 45° angle at which you viewed the treetop. If the string is hanging straight down and is covering the 45° angle line, the string is at a 45° angle to the straw. Standing upright, the tree makes a right angle (90° angle) with the ground. If you hold the protractor so you see the top of the tree when the string is hanging over the 45° angle mark, you are seeing the top of the tree at a 45° angle as well. The height of the tree and the distance you are away from the tree are equal lengths. You needed to make a small correction by adding your height because you aren't holding your protractor at ground level; then you had the height of the tree.

Bringing Up Baby

Did you or your parent ever plant two identical seedlings or vegetables, only to see one grow taller than another? Let's see if we can discover one reason that this happens.

WHAT YOU NEED

- 2 identical young plants: hot pepper plants, snapdragons, zucchinis, or any other type of garden annual*
- plant food
- potting soil
- trowel or scoop
- 2 identical plant pots, a little larger than the ones the plants are in
- felt-tipped pen
- paper for label
- measuring cup
- adult helper
- large jar or other container for plant food mixed with water
- container with plain water

*Get two that are the same size and the same kind, for example two pepper plants, each 5" (12.5 cm) tall.

WHAT YOU DO

1. Fill the empty pots with potting soil, and place one of the two young plants in each empty pot. If necessary, get an adult to help you to remove them from their old pots.

2. Put the plants next to each other in a sunny spot, or in whatever place your plant likes (according to its growing instructions) and label one plant FOOD and one NO FOOD.

3. Have an adult helper prepare a jar or other container with plant food mixed in water. Follow the mixing instructions on the plant food package.

4. Water the plant getting NO FOOD with plain tap water. Water the plant getting FOOD with the prepared plant food. Give each the same amount of liquid. Label your jar of plant food water and save the extra so you will have it when you need to water the plants again.

5. For a month or so, keep watering the plants every time they need water, as you did in Step 4. Can you see a difference between the two plants?

WHAT HAPPENED

The plant that received the water with plant food in it grew bigger than the plant that was given plain water. Like you, plants need **nutrients** (things that feed them) in order to grow. Not all plants are lucky enough to have someone feed them the correct diet. They have to get their food from the ground around them. What exactly is this food? Plant food is made of chemicals containing nitrogen, phosphorus, and potassium.

● ● ● ● ● ● ● ● ● ● ● ● ● ● ● ● ● ● ● ●

Natural Plant Food

You can make natural plant food in the form of compost. Compost is made from plant materials that have been allowed to break down. Worms play an important part in the breakdown of plant matter in compost. They eat the decaying organic material such as leaves and grass and recycle it through their bodies. The resulting product is rich in the nutrients that plants need to grow.

● ● ● ● ● ● ● ● ● ● ● ● ● ● ● ● ● ● ● ●

I'm Frond of You

Imagine you were a dinosaur living 400 million years ago. Presuming you were a plant eater, what do you think you would have been dining on? During the time of the dinosaurs, the forests were filled with giant ferns. Ferns are pretty strange when you compare them with other plants in your garden. Unlike poppies or sweet peas, ferns don't have seeds; they grow from spores.

☘ WHAT YOU NEED

- a fern frond* with little brown dots on the underside
- plastic sealable bag
- small shallow plastic container
- potting soil
- water
- plastic knife or scissors
- plant mister or spray bottle
- adult helper
- * A frond is a large leaf with many little leaflets on it.

WHAT YOU DO

1. In the spring or summer, ask an adult to help you find some ferns growing outdoors. The best place to look is in a dark or damp forested place. Turn over the fern fronds and look for

one with lots of specks of brown on the bottom. Those brown specks are the **sporangia,** special structures on ferns for holding spores. **Spores** are the reproductive cells of the fern.

2. Cut off the frond with the sporangia, put the frond in a plastic bag, and take it home. Allow the frond to dry in its bag on a counter overnight.

3. Place some potting soil in a small container and add enough water to make the soil damp, but not soggy.
4. Carefully hold the frond so that the dark specks are facing down over the soil, and shake the frond to release the spores. Do not add more soil or cover the spores.

Fern with sporangia.

5. Move the container to a dark, damp, warm place like the basement and watch the container over the next few days. Do not put the container near a window or in the sun. Mist the soil to keep it damp.
6. When tiny green structures appear, move your container to a brighter room, but not out into direct sunlight.

WHAT HAPPENED

In a few days, the spores started to grow, and tiny flat green leaflike plants called **gametophytes** appeared on the soil. These are the next step in the fern life cycle. Later they will grow to produce structures that contain the eggs and sperm of the fern. Traveling by water, a sperm joins an egg to grow into a new large fern plant like the one you saw in the forest when you first picked the frond.

Sticky Story

If you ever cut yourself, you probably remember that the cut bled a little bit, and then your skin formed a scab. You may have put a bandage over your cut. But what if you were a plant? How would you protect yourself when you were injured?

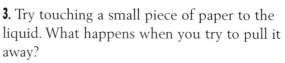

WHAT YOU NEED

- trees such as pine or maple
- small stick or twig
- paper
- magnifying glass
- adult helper
- pine cone with gooey clumps of resin on the outside (optional)

*Warning: Do not taste the resin you collect.

WHAT YOU DO

1. Take a close look at several different kinds of trees. Can you see any yellow, thick liquid oozing from a tree? Use a stick to scrape off some of the liquid. Do not use a sharp object, as it can harm the tree.

2. Place a dab of the liquid from the tree on a piece of paper. Look at the liquid with the magnifying glass. Do you see any bits of plant material or insects trapped in the liquid?

3. Try touching a small piece of paper to the liquid. What happens when you try to pull it away?

4. If you have a pine cone with resin, look at some resin from a pine cone under the magnifying glass.

What do maple trees and pancakes have in common? Maple syrup! Maple syrup is made from sap collected from sugar maple trees in the spring, when the warmer weather causes the sugary sap to flow. A hole is drilled into the tree and a tap is inserted. The sap comes out of the tap and is collected in a bucket. When there is enough sap in the bucket, it is boiled until it makes syrup. It takes about 45 gallons of sap to make one gallon of maple syrup (or 45 L to make 1 L of syrup). Only sugar maple trees yield the sap that makes syrup.

5. Wash your hands with soap and water after you have touched the resin.

WHAT HAPPENED

The thick liquid you collected is **resin.** It started out life as **sap,** in a very loose and liquid form. Sap is the colorless liquid that moves throughout the tree, carrying nutrients and water to the whole plant. You won't see the sap unless you break a twig or cut the tree deep enough for the sap to flow. The yellow liquid or hard stuff on the outside of the tree is resin. Resin is a tree's way of protecting itself when it is attacked by bugs or disease. Resin oozes out of the tree through a crack or comes out when the tree is damaged. The resin becomes thicker as it dries out in the air; it is often quite sticky. You may have noticed that the resin you collected makes pretty good glue. You might even have found an insect trapped in your resin sample.

DRAGON'S BLOOD

A scientist at the University of Calgary, in Alberta, Canada, has been studying the sap from a South American tree called the *Croton lechleri*. Commonly called *sangre de grado* or blood of the dragon, the red sap has been used by natives for hundreds of years for its healing powers. When people placed the sap from this kind of tree on a wound, they found that it cut down on infections and stopped or eased the pain. Scientists hope to create new drugs using this sap.

Insect Attractor

You may think flowers are pretty, but they aren't being pretty just for you. Flowers attract insects with their beautifully colored petals, lovely scents, and tasty nectar. In return, insects like bees and butterflies help flowers to make new plants. Let's see what's going on inside a simple flower.

🐞 WHAT YOU NEED

- several different kinds of flower, such as poppies, daisies, petunias, roses, coneflowers, hibiscus, geraniums, dandelions, or clover
- plastic knife
- paper
- magnifying glass
- tweezers
- adult helper

Note: If you are allergic to flowers or pollen, you should skip this activity.

WHAT YOU DO

1. Ask an adult to help you choose some flowers. Be sure no one minds that you cut them.

2. Pluck or cut each flower 2" or 3" (5 or 7 cm) down the stem from the bottom of the flower head. Place the flower on a flat surface. Look at the flower from the top and from the sides. Have an adult help you use a knife to slice the flower

in half down through the center, so you have two identical sections. For very small flowers, just pull them apart gently with the tweezers.

3. Use small tweezers to separate the different parts of the flower, and examine these sections under a magnifying glass. Compare the parts of the flower to the diagram shown here. Can you find all these parts on your flower?

4. Try Steps 1 through 3 again, this time using a different kind of flower.

5. Throw away the flower parts and wash your hands with soap and water when you are done.

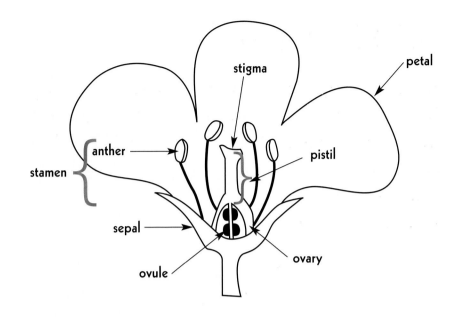

WHAT HAPPENED

You saw that flowers are made of several parts. The stem attaches the flower to the rest of the plant. Nutrients and water travel through the stem. There are often small green leaves called **sepals** attached to the stem just beneath the petals. The **petals** attract insects and give them a platform on which to stand while drinking nectar. In the center of the petals, you may have found two different types of tubelike structures. One is the female part of the plant or **pistil,** with the rounded **stigma** at the top, connected to the fatter **ovary** at the bottom. The ovary contains **ovules** (baby seeds). The ovary is the container in which the seeds develop. The other tubelike structures in the flower are the **stamens,** the male parts of the flower. Stamens produce **pollen** grains on their anthers at their tips. If you hold up a

flower and blow on the **anthers,** you will see small specks of pollen (usually yellow dust) going into the air. Pollen contains the male sperm cells of the flower. Pollen from one plant is carried onto the stigma of another plant by a bee or other insect or bird, or by the wind. When the pollen reaches the stigma, it forms a long tube through which the sperm cells can travel down into the ovary, where they meet with the ovules to form new seeds. Flowers come in many shapes and sizes. Some flowers don't have all the parts described above. Some flowers have many small blossoms grouped together, instead of one big blossom.

Make a Flower Press

Here's a way to enjoy the flowers of summer, even when summer is gone.

WHAT YOU NEED

- small flowers such as cornflower, daisies, primrose, miniature roses, geraniums, pansies, viola, poppies, sweet peas, violets, or dwarf marigolds
- large phone book*
- 3 or 4 heavy books
- clean newsprint paper, 6 or 8 pieces, letter size or bigger
- glue
- note cards
- adult helper

*Use last year's phone book in case it gets stained.

WHAT YOU DO

1. Ask an adult to help you select flowers. Pick flowers in the late morning when the dew has dried and the flowers are their freshest. Place the flowers someplace cool.

2. Select flowers of similar size or thickness to be pressed at the same time. Open the phone book to a page near the middle. Place 3 or 4 sheets of newsprint on top of the page. Place the flowers or leaves on top of the newsprint paper.

You may put the flowers face up, or face down.

3. Add several more sheets of newsprint on top of the flowers and close the phone book. If you have more flowers, you can do this again, opening to a different section of the phone book.

4. Place the phone book on the floor or someplace where you can leave it undisturbed for several weeks. Pile three or four heavy books on top of the

phone book to weight it down.

5. Depending on the kinds of flowers you used, it might take several weeks for the flowers to dry. Small flowers like pansies may be ready in a few days, but larger ones like dahlias or daisies might take longer.

6. Gently remove the flowers when they have dried, and glue them onto note cards or bookmarks, or use them for decorating other things.

Bean Swimmin'

Take a walk around your backyard or neighborhood and look at the plants that grow in different areas. Some plants grow better in full sunlight, some in shade. Other things influence the growth of plants. Soil conditions are important. In some areas, especially near the ocean, soil can have a high salt content. What would that do to plants? Let's see.

WHAT YOU NEED

- 2 plastic or paper cups
- salt
- water
- measuring cup
- measuring spoon
- 12 or more bean seeds (beans for sprouting, such as green peas, soy beans, or mung beans)
- plastic wrap
- paper towels
- 2 sealable plastic bags
- masking tape
- pencil

2. Place half of the bean seeds in each cup. Cover each cup loosely with a piece of plastic wrap; leave the cups overnight so the seeds can soak.

WHAT YOU DO

1. Pour ½ cup (125 mL) of water into each of the two plastic or paper cups. Add 2 tablespoons (30 mL) of salt to one of the cups, and use a spoon to stir the salt until it is completely dissolved. Label each cup so you know which is which, SALT or NO SALT, using the masking tape and pencil.

3. Next day, take a piece of paper towel and place the beans from the salt water cup on top of it. Wrap the towel loosely around the beans and moisten it with water from the cup. It should be damp but not dripping. Place the towel and beans inside a sealable plastic bag. Label it SALT.
4. Repeat Step 3 for the second cup of beans, using the water with no salt, and label its bag NO SALT.
5. Leave the plastic bags in a warm place for 2 or 3 days. Rinse the beans each day and return them to a paper towel moistened with either salty or unsalty water. Then look to see which set of beans grew the most.

WHAT HAPPENED

When you left the bean seeds in the damp paper towel, they began to **germinate,** or start to grow. The first step of germination is the swelling of the seeds, caused by their taking in some of the water surrounding them through their outer layer. The seeds that were in the salty water didn't swell up as much as the ones in the plain water. The movement of water into the seed happens because of something called **osmosis.** Water passed through a very thin tissue, in this case, the seed coat on the outside of the bean. In osmosis, water moves from an area where there are few salts or other dissolved materials to an area where there are more dissolved salts. The water that had more salt in it didn't move into the seeds as well as the plain water did.

Many plants don't grow in salty soil because they can't absorb enough water. If you live in an area where the soil is salty, you may need to grow plants in pots of soil brought from somewhere else or find plants that grow well in salty soil.

How Old Am I?

It's easy to find out how old you are. You can ask your parents your age or you can look on your birth certificate to see the date you were born. But how do you know how old some of the trees in your yard are? You can't ask the tree, but there is a way to estimate its age.

WHAT YOU NEED

- tree
- measuring tape or long piece of cord and ruler
- marker
- pen
- paper
- helper

WHAT YOU DO

1. Find a large tree, at least as tall as your parents, and wrap your measuring tape around the widest part of the trunk of the tree. You might need someone to help you with this step. Note the distance around the tree (the circumference) and write it down on the paper. (If you don't have a measuring tape, use a long cord to wrap around the tree and mark off the tree's circumference on the cord with a marker. Then measure the distance to the mark with your ruler.)

2. If you measured the circumference in inches, that measurement is also the approximate age of the tree in years. If you measured the circumference of the tree in centimeters, divide the circumference by 2.5 to find the age of the tree in years.

WHAT HAPPENED

You can estimate the age of a tree by measuring its circumference. Growth occurs just under the bark of the tree in a layer called the **cambium.** Each spring and summer, a new growth layer is added, and the tree gets fatter. The circumference of most trees grows by about 1" (2.5 cm) every year. Sadly, this formula doesn't work for all trees. Some trees, like firs and redwoods, may grow more than this in a year; others, like cedars, may grow less.

TRY THIS

The next time you see a tree stump, take a close look at the rings on the stump where the tree was cut. If you count the number of rings on the stump, you can tell how old the tree was when it was felled. The pattern of rings on the tree stump also tells us a little about the weather in the years in which the tree was growing. There are thicker rings added to the tree in the years when it had lots of water and sunshine. In dry years or years with poor weather, the rings added are thinner.

Plant a Tree

Here's a fun activity that will also do something good for the environment. Buy a small sapling such as a small fir tree or another tiny tree. Some companies give them away on Earth Day. Plant the tree in a nice open space and watch it grow. Water it from time to time if the weather is dry.

Stumpy

Stumpy is the enormous cross-section of a Canadian red cedar, which is mounted in the Biological Sciences building at the University of British Columbia, in Vancouver, B. C., Canada. The tree was cut down over 50 years ago and was given to the university to study. Scientists believe the tree was over 775 years old at the time it was felled. The original specimen weighed over 1290 lbs (585 kg) and was over 6.5' (2 m) in diameter.

That's Swell

When you want to plant a bush or a flower, you need a shovel or something sharp to break through the earth and dig a hole in the garden. How do tiny seeds manage to do the same thing without your help?

WHAT YOU NEED

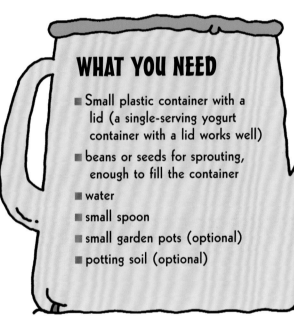

- Small plastic container with a lid (a single-serving yogurt container with a lid works well)
- beans or seeds for sprouting, enough to fill the container
- water
- small spoon
- small garden pots (optional)
- potting soil (optional)

WHAT YOU DO

1. Fill the plastic container with beans, and add enough water to cover the beans.

2. Place a lid on the container, and leave the container on the kitchen counter for a day or two. Watch what happens to the beans and the container.

3. Once the beans have germinated (started to grow), gently pull the sides of a bean apart and look inside.

4. When the beans have sprouted, you can plant each one in its own small pot if you want to. Fill the pots with soil, poke holes twice the depth of the bean in the soil, and stick a bean each hole. Cover it with soil. Keep the pots moist, and place them in a warm, sunny spot. When the bean plants are 6" to 8" tall (15 to 20 cm) tall, they can be transplanted into the garden.

WHAT HAPPENED

The beans in the container of water absorbed the water and swelled until they were much larger than their original size. They may have swelled up enough to pop the lid right off of the container. When bean seeds are planted in the ground, they also absorb water. This starts the germination process. The seed has a tough seed coat, which splits. The tiny cells that make up the plant begin to split apart to make new cells. A tiny plant forms inside the bean seed and bursts outwards. The root grows out from one end. From the other end of the bean seed, the young seedling begins to emerge.

The curved green part you see at the top of the seedling is called the **hypocotyl.** It pokes out of the bean first; then it uncurls and the **cotyledons** or seed leaves poke out. The **epicotyl,** carrying the first foliage leaves, grows up from between the cotyledons. The bean seed acts as a food source for the new plant, feeding it until it develops enough roots and leaves to feed itself from the soil.

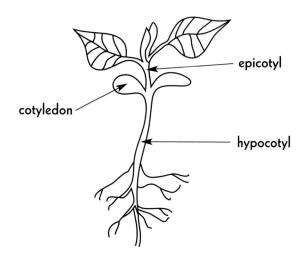

Bean sprout

Sundial

If you don't have a watch, how can you tell when it's time to go home for lunch? Other than that grumbly sound your tummy makes, is there another way to judge if it's noon?

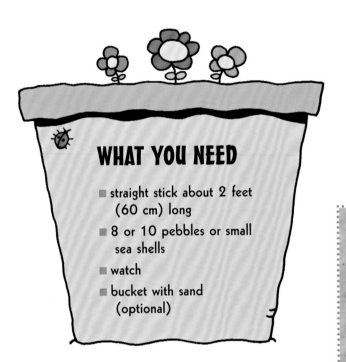

WHAT YOU NEED

- straight stick about 2 feet (60 cm) long
- 8 or 10 pebbles or small sea shells
- watch
- bucket with sand (optional)

WHAT YOU DO

1. Find a sunny spot and push the stick upright into the grass or earth. If your yard doesn't have any grass or earth, fill a small bucket with sand and place the stick in the bucket. The sand will hold the stick erect.

2. Start in the morning when the sun is up. At each hour (7:00 am, 8:00 am, 9:00 am, etc.), use a pebble to mark the place where the end of the stick's shadow falls. Keep coming back every hour that there is daylight to do this.

3. At the end of the day you will have made a sundial.

WHAT HAPPENED

The shadow cast by the stick changes position and length as the sun moves (really "appears to move") across the sky. The shadow will fall near the pebbles you have placed at about the same time each day for a few weeks. This allows you to tell the time. The lengths of the shadows will change throughout the year. In the summer, the shadows are shorter; in the winter the shadow are longer.

Sundials and clocks both tell time, but they don't measure the same thing. Sundials tell you what time it is by the position of the sun. Noon on a sundial is when the sun is at the highest point in the sky for that day. The shortest shadow is cast when it is noon. The term a.m. stands for *ante meridiem*, before noon. *Post meridiem* or p. m. refers to the afternoon, the time after the sun has passed its highest point.

Rings & Things

Take a walk in a garden and look closely at the centers of flowers and the leaves on plants and trees. Do you see any patterns in the way the leaves are arranged, or does it all look pretty random? Could math have anything to do with the shapes and patterns in the world around us?

🐞 WHAT YOU NEED

- large pinecone with flat bottom (such as one from a bristle cone pine)
- watercolors or 4 or 5 different colors of nail polish that are easy to tell apart
- egg cup or hunk of modeling clay
- sticky substance like Fun-tac™
- whole pineapple
- about 30 pieces of thin ribbon or colored paper, ¼" x 15" (½ x 38 cm) each, in 4 or 5 colors
- large sunflower
- pen and paper

WHAT YOU DO

1. Look closely at the center part of the sunflower. Do the seeds form a pattern?

2. Find 2 large, open pinecones that are about the same shape and size. Place each pinecone upside down in an egg cup, so the pointed end of the pinecone is inside the cup. This will make it easier to color the pinecone.

5. Try the following activity using a pineapple. Starting up near the leaves, use something sticky like Fun-Tac or modeling clay to tack a ribbon onto the pineapple scales to mark one spiral going around the pineapple in a clockwise direction. Use a different color of ribbon for the next clockwise spiral. Keep going until you have marked all the spirals in the clockwise direction. Then try tacking ribbons on the spirals going in the counterclockwise direction on the same pineapple. How many spirals does the pineapple have in each direction?

Pinecone with counter-clockwise spirals painted

3. Start from the center of the bottom of the pinecone, and use one color of paint or nail polish to paint one of the curved lines going in the clockwise direction on one of the pinecones. Use different colors of paint or nail polish to mark each of the curved lines moving out from the center point **(spirals)** that are going in the clockwise direction on that pine cone. When you are done marking all the spirals, count them. How many spirals did the pinecone have in the clockwise direction?

4. On the second pinecone, repeat step 3, but paint all the spirals going in the counterclockwise direction.

WHAT HAPPENED

You probably noticed some spiral patterns, which are found in plants and flowers and in many other things in nature. For example, the pinecone in the picture has 13 spirals turning right or clockwise and 8 spirals turning left, or counterclockwise. The pineapple scales were arranged in 8 spirals going in one direction and 13 spirals going in the opposite direction. 8 and 13 are two numbers in a mathematical pattern called the Fibonacci sequence. Scientists have been studying these patterns for over 300 years.

Did You Know?

The Fibonacci sequence is one of the easiest mathematical formulas you will ever learn. The sequence is 1, 2, 3, 5, 8, 13, 21, 34, 55, 89, etc.

$$1 + 1 = 2$$
$$1 + 2 = 3$$
$$2 + 3 = 5$$
$$3 + 5 = 8$$

Do you see a pattern here? The next number is 13 (5 + 8 = 13), and so on. In the Fibonacci sequence, each number is equal to the sum of the two numbers that went before it. Keep adding the last number to the one before it, and you have the sequence. Spirals aren't found only in plants. Mollusks (for example, snails) have spiral patterns on their shells; even the galaxy where we live, the Milky Way, is a spiral galaxy.

The study of the arrangement of leaves on a stem is called **phyllotaxis.** It turns out that new growth on a plant tends to occur at a particular angle, because it will have the most room that way. A new leaf will grow in the biggest space available on the end of a shoot. Taken together, the leaves end up growing in a radial or spiral pattern. This is true for pinecone scales and pineapple scales as well.

Spiral pattern in the center of a flower.

Breakdown

Would you like to be green? No, not green like a frog. Green, in this case, is a term meaning "friendly to the environment or the world around you." Here's a simple experiment to help you think about how to help the environment.

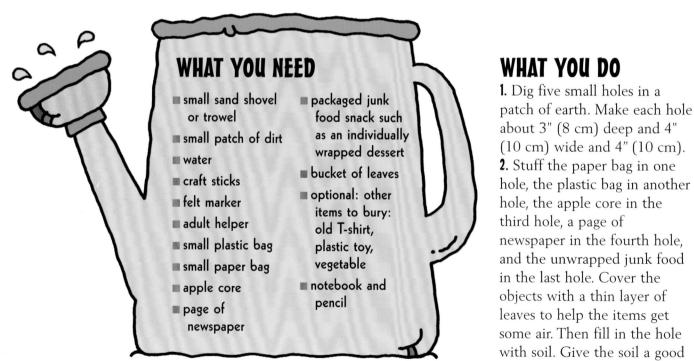

WHAT YOU NEED

- small sand shovel or trowel
- small patch of dirt
- water
- craft sticks
- felt marker
- adult helper
- small plastic bag
- small paper bag
- apple core
- page of newspaper
- packaged junk food snack such as an individually wrapped dessert
- bucket of leaves
- optional: other items to bury: old T-shirt, plastic toy, vegetable
- notebook and pencil

WHAT YOU DO

1. Dig five small holes in a patch of earth. Make each hole about 3" (8 cm) deep and 4" (10 cm) wide and 4" (10 cm).
2. Stuff the paper bag in one hole, the plastic bag in another hole, the apple core in the third hole, a page of newspaper in the fourth hole, and the unwrapped junk food in the last hole. Cover the objects with a thin layer of leaves to help the items get some air. Then fill in the hole with soil. Give the soil a good watering.

the same as it did when you first buried it. Some plastic bags contain materials that help them biodegrade or break down, while others don't break down. Which kind was your plastic bag? And, while it's not appetizing to think of it, some processed food contains so many chemical preservatives that it also will not rot or biodegrade easily. What did your junk food look like?

3. Use a craft stick to mark each hole, labeling it with what you've put inside. Record the date you placed the items in the holes.
4. Dig up the items after 2 weeks, 4 weeks and 6 weeks to see what has happened to them. After digging them up and looking at them, rebury them. Which items seem to be in the same condition as when you put them in the hole? Which items have changed?
5. Wash your hands with soap and water after you have finished digging in the garden.

WHAT HAPPENED

Over time, the first item to change was probably the apple. It was eaten by insects, worms, and other creatures or it simply decayed or rotted away.

The newspaper and paper bag fell apart next. These items were made from wood fibers, which were easily broken down. Your plastic bag probably looked pretty much

Did You Know?

Some things biodegrade or break down quickly, so there is nothing left of them in a landfill or in a garbage dump. Some things (for example, certain kinds of plastics) never break down and will always stay in their original condition. The average family in the United States throws away about 500 plastic garbage bags a year. This can really add up over time. Cutting down on the number of packaged items you buy and carrying your groceries in reusable bags can help reduce the amount of garbage and make the environment a better place.

Life Cycle

Life cycle sounds like a great name for a piece of exercise equipment, but in this book it means that living things are born, grow to maturity, have offspring, and die. Some plants go through this cycle quickly; others can live for hundreds of years. Let's look at a year in the life of a tree or bush.

WHAT YOU NEED

■ camera
■ tree or bush that loses its leaves in fall
■ flowering plant such as marigold
■ magnifying glass

WHAT YOU DO

1. Choose a green tree or bush, the kind that loses its leaves in winter. A fruit tree or a flowering tree like a magnolia is a good choice, or a flowering bush that grows each year, such as rosebush or hydrangea.

2. Take a photo of the same bush or tree on the same date each month for 12 months.
3. Create a poster with the pictures you have taken. How did the plant change throughout the year?
4. Look at a plant that grows more rapidly; for example, a marigold. Take a picture of its bud, flower, and seeds and look at them closely. Save some seeds and see if you can grow them the next spring.

WHAT HAPPENED

You saw a year in the life cycle of a bush or tree. In the spring, buds began to open on the bare branches, and small flowers appeared. The tree or bush may have been covered with flowers. As the weather got warmer, the tree or bush began to grow taller and had more branches and leaves covering it. By summer, the tree had a full crown of leaves, and it may have borne beautiful fruit. In the fall, as the weather got cooler, the fruit fell from the tree. The leaves began to change color and fall from the tree also. By the time the first snowfall came, the branches were bare and the tree was ready for a winter nap. You can follow the life cycle of an annual plant also, even in a marigold plant that you grow in a container.

Biodiversity in Your Own Backyard

What is biodiversity and what is it doing in my backyard? Biodiversity is a measure of the number of different species (kinds of living things) that exist in a location. A good place to start to learn more about biodiversity is right nearby.

WHAT YOU NEED

- pencil
- notebook
- natural history books, such as field guides to birds, plants and trees
- adult helper or friend

WHAT YOU DO

1. Find a comfy spot in the garden where you can sit, or take a walk in the park. Write down all the different living things that you see. Don't just write BIRD, use a field guide to try to identify the kind of bird. Take a note of how many of each kind of creature or other living thing you see.

2. Take a closer look. Did you see any insects? What about animals or plants in pools or streams of water?

Bee

3. Next time you are on a bus or in a car, look out the window and take note of the area around you. What kinds of living things do you see? Is the landscape different from the one near your home?

WHAT HAPPENED

You probably saw many different types of animals and  plants, depending on where you live or where you went to make your observations. The animals and plants all have different roles to play in their environment. Some living things such as plants are producers, creating food. Animals are consumers, eating the plants or smaller animals. You may have seen small soil animals, the decomposers. All of these living things have to work together for a healthy environment. If any of them is missing, the others will suffer. The more species that live in an area, the healthier that environment is.

Hibiscus flower with anole

Cicada

Snail

Orchid

It's Your Planet

Although you may see many plants and animals when you look out your window, in large parts of the world plants and animals are being destroyed at a rapid rate. What can you do to help protect biodiversity? Check with your school or local community organizations to see if you can plant a specimen garden of native trees and shrubs in your area. See if local gardeners or gardening clubs will donate plants or help you find some. That will help ensure that the many birds, insects and other living things that need those plants to survive won't lose their habitat.

Glossary

abdomen: in an insect, the third main part of the body. In a spider it is the second part of the body.

annelids: a group of segmented worms, which includes earthworms and leeches.

anole: a slender lizard 5" to 8" (12 to 20 cm) long that has large toe pads. The green anole is usually green but can change to brown. The green anoles are native to the southern United States, but have been introduced in other places as well.

anther: pollen-carrying portion of the stamen of a flower.

aphids: small insects that drink the sap of plants.

arachnids: group of animals that includes spiders, ticks, and scorpions. Arachnids have 8 legs and two main body parts.

arthropods: group of animals with jointed legs and a thick, strong, flexible outer layer called the exoskeleton, which supports the body. Some examples are spiders, lobsters, and insects.

barbicels: tiny hooklike structures on the barbules of a bird's feather, which hold the feather parts in shape.

barbs: primary branches off the central shaft of contour and flight feathers.

barbules: microscopic branches off the barbs of a bird's feather.

biodegradable: capable of decaying through the action of living things (for example, microbes).

biodiversity: the variety of life, including the many different kinds of species, habitats, and ecosystems in a place.

cambium: a thin layer of growth tissue between the bark and the wood of trees and woody shrubs.

camouflage: protective disguise of many animals, which makes them hard to see in their natural surroundings.

caterpillar: larval stage of a butterfly or moth.

cephalothorax: combined head and thorax that is the upper body section of a spider.

compost: a mixture of rotted plant material used by gardeners to give nutrients to plants.

contour feathers: body feathers that give the bird its shape and color.

cotyledon: seed leaf of a flowering plant.

dicot: short for dicotyledon; flowering plant whose seedlings have two seed leaves (cotyledons).

down feathers: soft, fluffy feathers that are found under the bird's contour feathers. They keep the bird warm.

embryo: the developing young of an animal or plant.

epicotyl: the portion of a plant seedling just above the seed leaves.

exoskeleton: tough, jointed outer skeleton found on the outer part of the body of arthropods such as insects, spiders, and crabs.

ferns: a group of flowerless green plants that have large leaves called fronds and reproduce by spores instead of by seeds.

Fibonacci sequence: sequence of numbers in which each number is equal to the sum of the two numbers that went before it.

filoplumes: very tiny feathers that have connections to nerve endings on the bird.

flight feathers: long, strong feathers found on a bird's wings and tail; they provide the power and lift so a bird can fly.

frond: a large leaf with many little leaflets on it.

gametophyte: in plants like ferns that have alternation of generations, the small plant that produces the egg and the sperm.

gastropods: animals like snails and slugs, which use a large muscular foot at the base of their bodies to glide forward slowly.

genetics: the study of heredity.

germinate: to start developing or growing.

habitat: the environment or place where a plant or animal normally lives and grows.

heredity: passing on of traits of living things to their offspring.

honeydew: sweet substance given off by aphids and some other insects.

hymenoptera: a group of insects that includes bees, wasps, and ants, which often live in large colonies. Their wings are thin and bend easily.

hypocotyl: the part of the sprout of a plant seedling that is just below the seed leaf or cotyledon. It will develop into the root.

insects: group of arthropods with 3 main body parts (head, thorax, and abdomen), six legs, and (usually) two sets of wings. Some examples are ants, butterflies, beetles, and house flies.

invertebrate: an animal that doesn't have a backbone. Examples are worms, slugs, insects, and spiders.

larva: an immature stage of any invertebrate, which is very different in appearance from the adult. For example, the caterpillar is a larval stage of a butterfly.

lubricant: a slippery substance that helps things slide along past each other.

mandibles: strong mouthparts of an insect or larva.

metamorphosis: the change of physical form, structure, or substance in an animal, which occurs after birth or hatching. The change of a caterpillar into a butterfly is an example of metamorphosis.

mollusks: a group of animals with soft bodies, often encased in shells. Mollusks include snails, clams, octopuses, oysters, and thousands of others.

molt: (verb) to shed hair, feathers, shell, or an outer layer of skin periodically.

monocots: short name for monocotyledon; seed plants whose sprouting seeds have one starting leaf each.

nectar: sweet liquid put forth by a plant, which attracts insects or birds.

nutrients: things that nourish a plant or animal.

offspring: child or young of a particular parent; descendant.

osmosis: movement of a solvent such as water across a membrane separating two solutions, to make the concentrations of dissolved materials on each side the same.

phyllotaxis: the arrangement of leaves on a stem, or the study of that arrangement.

pollen: fine grains produced in the anthers of flowering plants, which contain the male sex cells.

predator: an animal that eats, or preys on, other animals.

proboscis: the long feeding tube of the butterfly.

pupa: encased stage in development of certain insects, which occurs between the larva and the adult stage.

radula: organ on the mouth of a mollusk (including a snail), that has sharp teeth, which scrape away food.

resin: a solid or partly solid substance given off by some trees (mostly pines and firs).

sap: the colorless liquid that moves throughout a tree or other plant, carrying nutrients and water to the whole plant.

seed: fertilized egg of a flowering plant. A seed has a seed coat and an embryo, the inner part that can develop into a new plant; it also contains food for the embryo.

shaft: central structure of a feather.

semiplume feathers: fuzzy feathers, larger than down feathers, that help keep birds warm.

setae: bristles on the underside of an earthworm.

species: a group of related living things that resemble one another and can breed among themselves but cannot breed successfully with other species. The species is the basic category of classification in biology.

spinnerets: silk-spinning glands found on the rear of a spider's abdomen.

sporangia: the specialized structures on some plants, such as ferns, that produce and hold spores.

spore: reproductive cell of a seedless plant such as a fern.

stamen: male organ of a flower. Its top part is the anther, which produces pollen grains.

symmetry: the correspondence in size, form, and arrangement of parts on opposite sides of a plane, line, or point.

synthetic: made by people, not naturally occurring.

thorax: in insects and other arthropods, the body division between the head and the abdomen. The legs are attached to the thorax.

vane: soft side parts of a feather, which grow out from the central shaft; they are made up of smaller parts called barbs.

ACKNOWLEDGMENTS

Our deepest thanks to John Ireland, manager at the Reifel Migratory Bird Sanctuary, for his expertise and assistance. Thanks also to Big Bob Meniece for being the ferryman on the Delta River and for his protection against fierce creatures. We are indebted to Pamela Dalgleish of Weyerhaeuser Company, Ltd. for her picture of the cross-section of the tree. And to Tom Crute of Home Hardware on West 10th in Vancouver. You are a true gentleman for lugging and arranging the clay pots. As always, where would we be without the assistance of the University of British Columbia? The wonderful photo of Stumpy was taken by Michelle Cooke, UBC Public Affairs, and was sent to us by Sharmini Thiagarajah. Dr. Elaine Humphrey: You know everything and you are amazing!

The editors thank the wonderful models for their help and patience.

Index